Kenya's Northern Frontier
and Far Beyond

Kenya's Northern Frontier and Far Beyond

MEMOIRS OF A DISTRICT OFFICER

HUGH WALKER MBE

Trenchant Books

StoryTerrace

Hardback privately published and printed by Story Terrace January 2020
10 White's Row, London E1 7NF
www.StoryTerrace.com

eBook published by Trenchant Books April 2020
8 Trenchard Street London SE10 9PA
www.trenchantbooks.com

This Paperback published by Trenchant Books September 2021
37 Durwent Close Plymouth PL9 9TP
www.trenchantbooks.com

A CIP catalogue record for this book is available from the British Library

eBook Mobi ISBN 978-0-9954766-3-9
Paperback ISBN 978-0-9954766-4-6

Text by Paddy Magrane, on behalf of Story Terrace, and Lesley Curwen
Original design by Grade Design and Adeline Media, London
eBook and Paperback formatted by Trenchant Books

CONTENTS

1   MY EARLY LIFE

My story begins in rather unusual circumstances. I was born on 15th February 1931, in Eltham, south London. My mother was an unmarried Welsh nurse called Muriel Rogers. Over the course of seven years, she gave birth to three children, including me, as a result of an affair with a married man, Hubert Archibald King, whom she had met on a train.

With the birth of each child, my mother hoped Hubert would be persuaded to leave his disabled wife. It never happened. So, she had each child adopted, separately. I did not discover I had siblings until many years later, when I was an adult.

I was the eldest of the three siblings and was named Peter Rogers on the birth certificate. A blank was left for the father's name.

Initially, Muriel placed me in a home for unwanted children at Wittersham, in Kent. It was run by a woman called Lillian Booth, who had a vicious temper. Lillian came from an upper-class family, but had married a train driver, a match that was considered to be beneath her. I might have languished under Lillian's care were it not for her two elderly spinster sisters, Florence and Violet Walker, who visited the home when I was aged about four. By all accounts, they were enchanted by me. "Oh, isn't he sweet" said Florence, who wanted to adopt me. The decision was made - apparently.

Muriel holding a baby (not me)

At the children's home, aged four

Things did not go smoothly. When the sisters arrived at the local adoption office on 23rd July 1935, it transpired that, at the age of 60, Florence was too old to adopt. Violet immediately seized control of the process. "Oh give me the pen," she said. "I'll sign the adoption papers."

From then on, I was 'hers'. She also called me Hugh instead of Peter, the name I'd been given at birth and which remained on my adoption certificate. I can't recall what I thought about it all – I was only four!

Curiously enough, it was my mother Muriel who took me from the children's home to my new home in Wadhurst, Sussex, where the Walkers lived. We were driven in the sisters' large Wolseley car by a uniformed chauffeur named George. I remember my mother was wearing a fur stole around her neck. When we arrived at the spinsters' house, Cockmount, in Jones Lane, she kissed me goodbye forever.

Aunt Florrie

2 LIFE WITH THE AUNTS

'Aunt Vi', as she became known, proved to be a stern disciplinarian, while Aunt Florrie was a sweet and affectionate old lady. She had a yappy Yorkshire terrier, Julia, and loved to bestow cuddles on the dog and me. Life in Wadhurst was Victorian, with a maid, Emily, and her brother, George the chauffeur and gardener, serving the big house. The servants were expected to call me 'Master Hugh'. At first, I did not go to school. I had an aged nanny called Miss Ward whom I did not like. I remember maliciously jumping up and down on her corns when we were out walking! Thankfully, she was replaced by a kind young governess, Doreen Cutbush, who taught me the three Rs and remained a friend later in life.

Aunt Vi liked to use phrases such as 'stiff upper lip', 'no molly-coddling', 'don't be a cry-baby', and 'up and doing little Christian' (the latter a ditty that has long since gone out of fashion, which goes on with the words, '…little Christian while 'tis day, do the work the Master gives you, do not linger by the way').

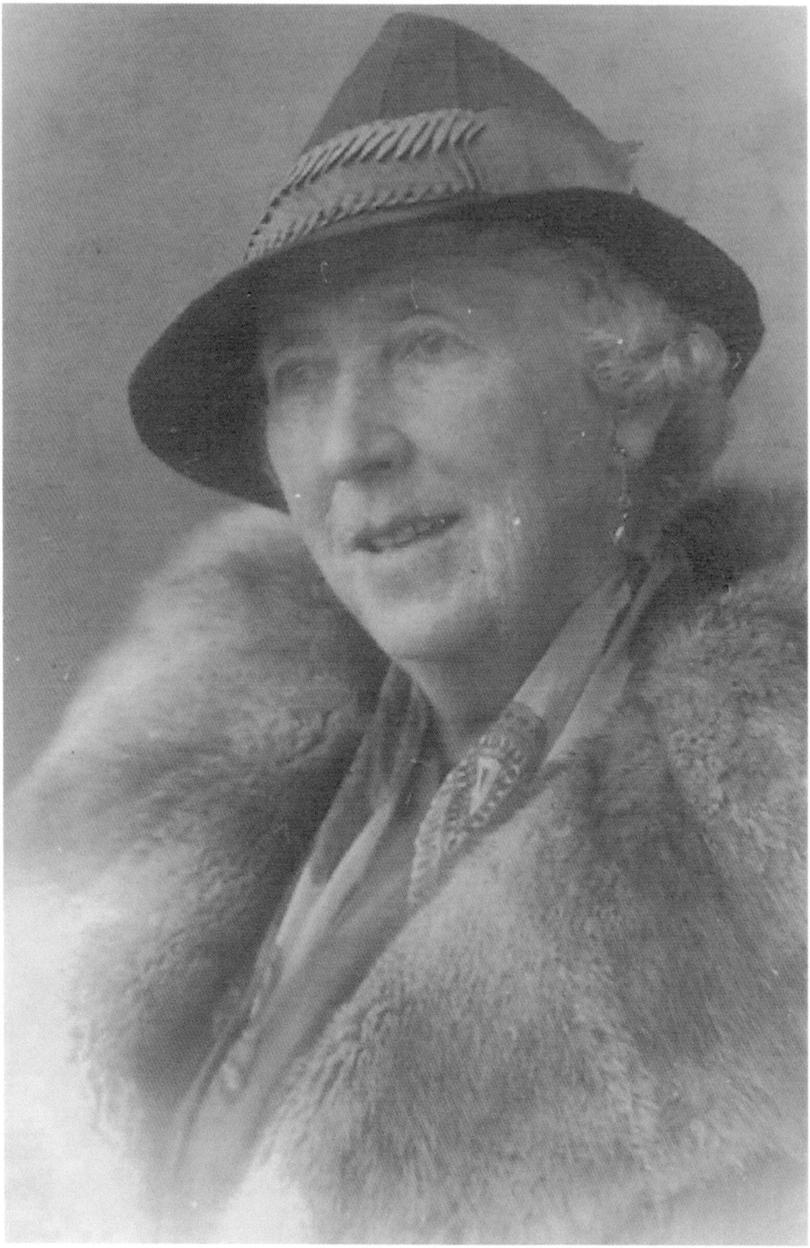

Aunt Vi

Vi had a collection of Hindustani phrases which she'd bellow, such as 'oolooka batcha – son of an owl!' or 'hut jow, jeldee jow' – get out, hurry up!' and 'bagga lagga hai Johnny wallah – get out of the way, Indian!' She had learned these from her soldier brothers while staying with them in India. The two sisters quarrelled fiercely over how I should be brought up. These arguments were so intense that Aunt Vi decided to move out, building her own wooden cottage, where I was to live with her, in the next-door field. I was allowed to go and see Aunt Florrie once a day for half an hour, at the end of which a dog whistle was blown to summon me back, with Aunt Vi waiting at the door.

It was hardly ideal for a small boy to be brought up by these elderly spinsters. Wars had deprived the Walker sisters of potential husbands, so they suffered unfulfilled lives as women. Aunt Vi was not a bad person and I believe she did her best. But she had grown up with repressive Victorian attitudes which she then projected on to her adopted son.

Eventually I was sent to a preparatory school, Boarzell, at Hurst Green in Sussex. My memories of this time are very happy. At last I had playmates, which made a huge difference.

In 1940, as the German bombing campaign intensified, Boarzell pupils were scheduled to be evacuated to the Lake District. Aunt Vi, who was frightened of bombs herself, decided to move with me to Westmorland to stay with a couple of artists she and Florrie had known when they lived in Wadhurst.

We arrived at the Bield, a 400-year-old farmhouse in the remote and beautiful valley of Little Langdale, a place which became a kind of spiritual home for me.

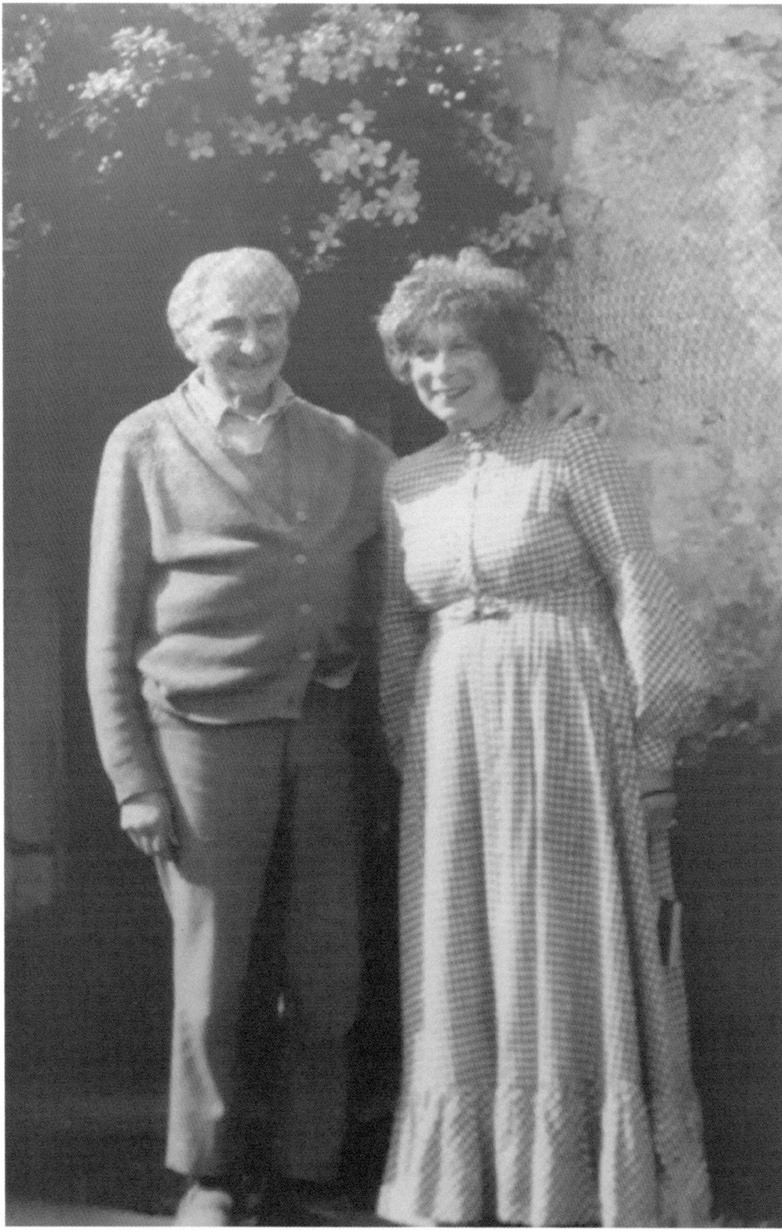

Delmar and Josefina

Our artist hosts were Delmar Banner, a renowned painter, and his sculptress wife Josefina de Vasconcellos, who became an important influence in my life.

I will never forget waking up in the Bield the morning after we arrived. I appeared to be surrounded by mountains, tarns, lakes and rivers. As my eyes adjusted, I realised these were Delmar's extraordinary murals. He had painted the walls with a stunning local panorama, executed from memory. Utterly beautiful.

After a fortnight, Aunt Vi moved us to Grasmere and then on to the leafy valley of Easedale, which became a rural 'Shangri-La' for me. We stayed with General Sir James and Lady Gay O'Dowda. I played with huge sets of model soldiers owned by the General.

I loved the Lake District. Wadhurst seemed dull in comparison. The mountains, waterfalls and lakes, in fact the whole panoply of nature, fascinated me. It was the first time I got a taste for the open-air life, which was to be a feature of much of my subsequent career.

Aunt Vi and I would ramble for hours on the fells. Despite being in her 70s, she was a sturdy walker. The war seemed far away, although I recall one night when I saw the sky turn red from fierce fires in distant Barrow-in-Furness, the aftermath of a German bombing raid.

This blissful existence was not to last. In 1944, we returned south to Wadhurst. Aunt Vi was determined that I should go to a public school. I was enrolled at Tonbridge School in Kent. I was a boarder for the first two years, an experience I enjoyed, not least because it got me away from home. But then Aunt Vi complained that she couldn't afford the fees, so I had to travel there daily by

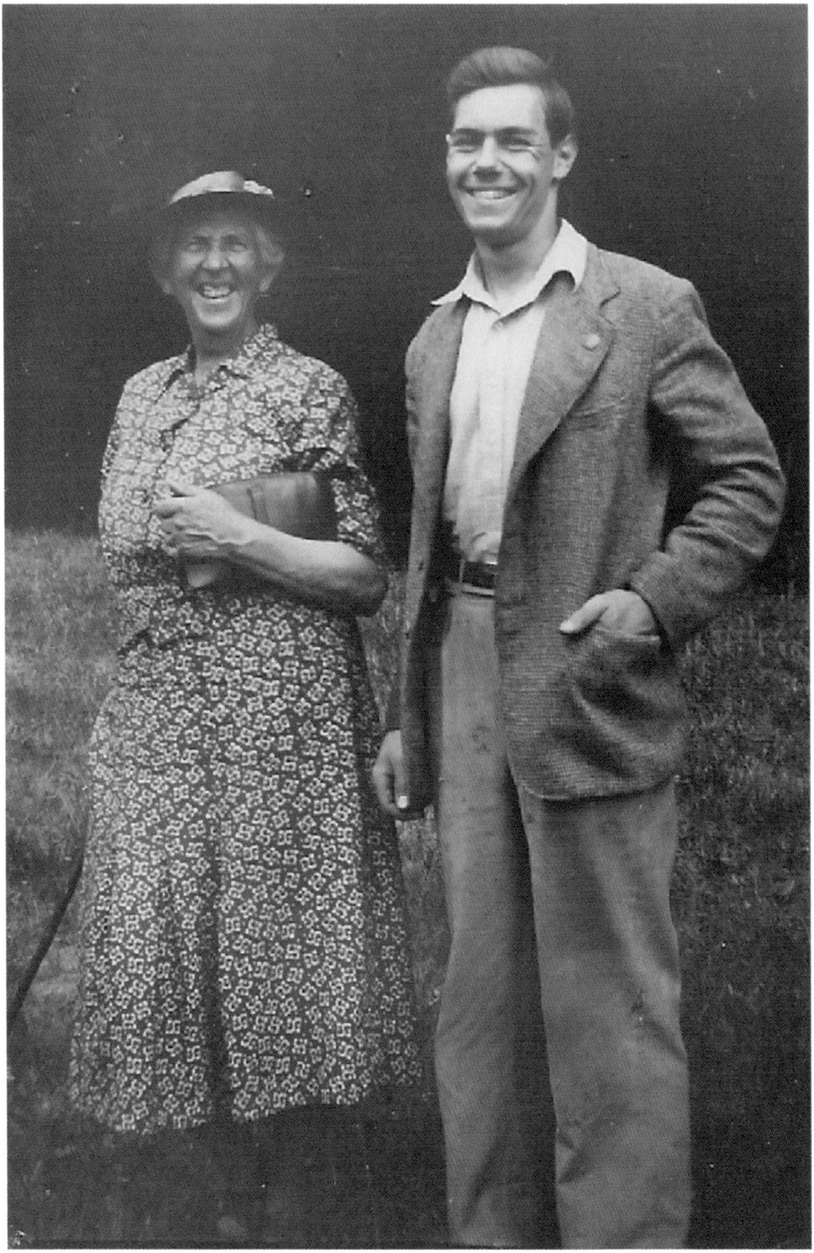

With Aunt Vi

bus.

I found languages and religious education easy, but geometry and algebra were difficult concepts for me to master. Possibly as a result of these gaps in my knowledge, I failed my school certificate, although I did achieve distinctions in German and French (my gift for languages was to serve me well in later life). Aunt Vi said I would have to get a job, but Delmar and Josefina kindly offered to pay for me to repeat a whole year in 1948. This time I passed!

At the age of 17, I got a temporary job with a local mushroom farmer, a Dutchman called Mr Visser. I had to plant mycelium on long trestle tables which sat under lights, and pick and box the mushrooms every day.

It filled in the time and earned me some money until, at the age of 18, I was called up for compulsory National Service, in my case with the Royal Artillery. I undertook basic training at Oswestry and was then sent to the Officer Cadet Training Unit (OCTU) at Eaton Hall. At the time, I never thought 'this army life is the life for me'. It was simply National Service, which everyone had to do.

The OCTU officers told me my maths was too poor for a gunnery officer, for which I would need to calculate heights and trajectories, so I was transferred instead to the infantry. I was sent to the Queen's Own Royal West Kent Regiment. But on arrival, I was informed they did not have a vacancy. There were several alternatives – one of which was to go to Africa. Something in me must have craved a far-flung destination, because the mere thought of Africa felt incredibly exciting. It was certainly preferable to square-bashing in England.

The decision was taken to post me to the 'Somaliland Scouts', a now long-disbanded regiment once known as the Somaliland Camel Corps. I was to be based in Hargeisa, Somaliland. It was a move that would change the course of my entire life and cement in me a lifelong love affair with Africa.

3 A NEW LIFE IN SOMALILAND

There was so much about my new role that was exciting. It was the first foreign trip of my life, for starters. I hadn't even been to Paris for the weekend so you can imagine my awe-struck face as I stepped off the plane into the arid heat of Hargeisa. Somaliland was a million miles from the world I'd left behind.

The Somaliland Scouts

The army encampment was based in a rural area – a landscape of bush and scrub, where there was sparse grazing. Camel country, in other words.

As second lieutenant in charge of a platoon, one of my duties was to take the soldiers into the reserved area of Ogaden, formerly part of Ethiopia, where the Americans were looking for oil and we were tasked with protecting the surveyors and drillers.

The Americans had not endeared themselves to the locals. Their bulldozers had knocked down a number of nut trees, a source of food, and the Somalis were not happy.

It took a little while to win the respect of some of the Americans, despite the protection we were offering them. One night, one of the guards at the camp in the Ogaden (and not a member of my platoon), deserted with his rifle across the border to Somalia. I remember how one of the American oil men muttered, "If your man deserts, you must be a chicken-shit officer!" This irked me. When their boss from Sinclair Oil in Addis Ababa visited and was introduced to me, I said boldly, "These are my soldiers and I am their chicken-shit officer". The oil men didn't know where to look. But after that, they conceded that I was, after all, a good guy who could clearly take a joke.

While I was with the Scouts, I adopted a young dog called Jimmy, who I grew very fond of. One night, my company commander, the monocled Major 'Baron' Hexter-Stabbins, mistook Jimmy for a 'pi-dog' (a wild scavenger) and shot him. I was deeply upset. On discovering his mistake – that the wild dog was in fact a tame pet – he apologised profusely.

By and large, my time in Somaliland was very enjoyable. This was, after all, peace-time. It was there that I learned some spoken Somali and discovered I had an aptitude for languages. In fact, noses were put out of joint when I came second in a Government Somali course, attended mostly by administrative officers with university degrees. At that point, I had no idea what to do after National Service. Out of the blue, my prowess in Somali, which was a very difficult language, led my superiors to suggest that I should apply to join the Colonial Service.

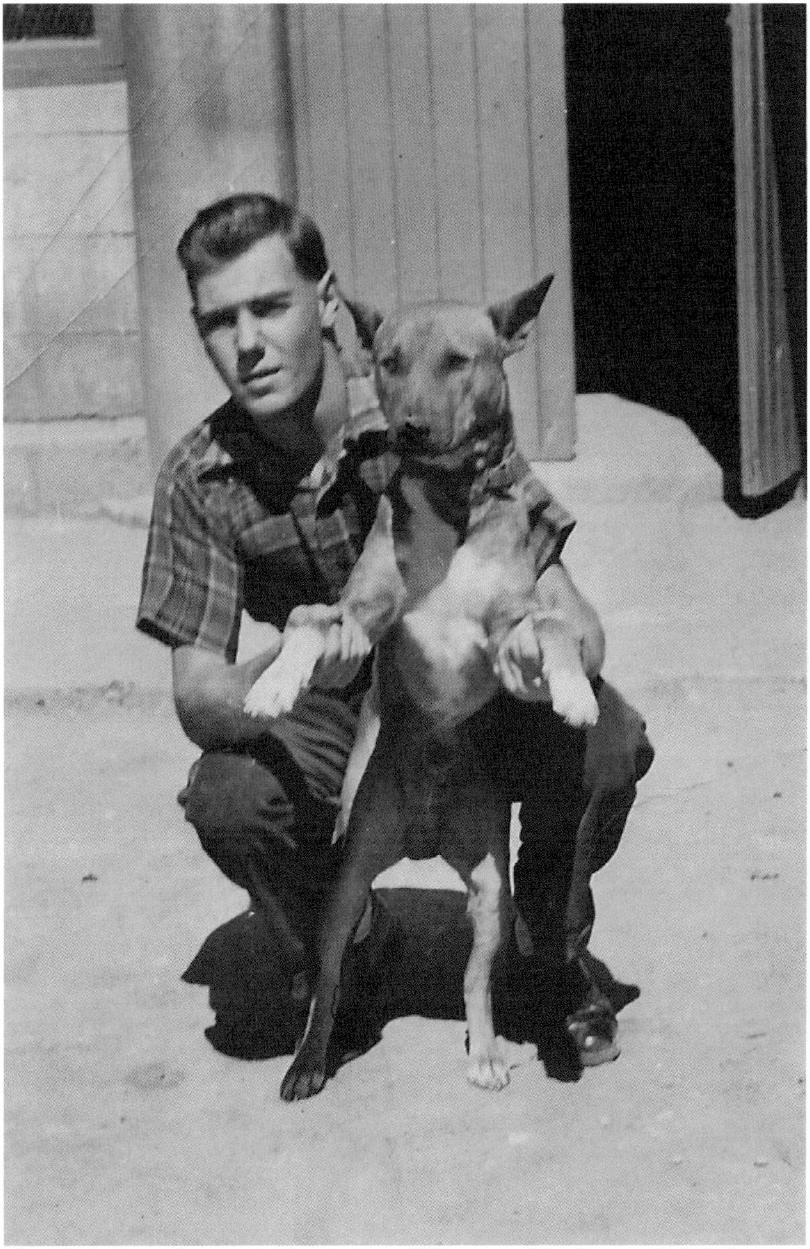

With Jimmy, 1950

Given my poor school certificate and lack of a degree, I never imagined I would even be considered. But I applied and, to my surprise, was accepted. In 1952, I was sent to Hertford College, Oxford University, for a year's academic training as a cadet.

At this news, I remember Aunt Vi was torn between pride at my success, and sadness that she would be left lonely in England once I headed abroad on a permanent basis.

Vi being Vi, imposed a condition – that if I entered the colonial service, I had to spend all my leaves with her. Naturally, I agreed. I was so desperate to get back to Africa.

At the end of an enjoyable year in Oxford, I expected to be sent back to Somaliland but instead, was posted to Kenya. It was 1953 and the Mau Mau uprising against the British was in full swing. Despite the potential dangers, I was absolutely delighted. Somaliland was a backwater. Kenya, by contrast, was a big country.

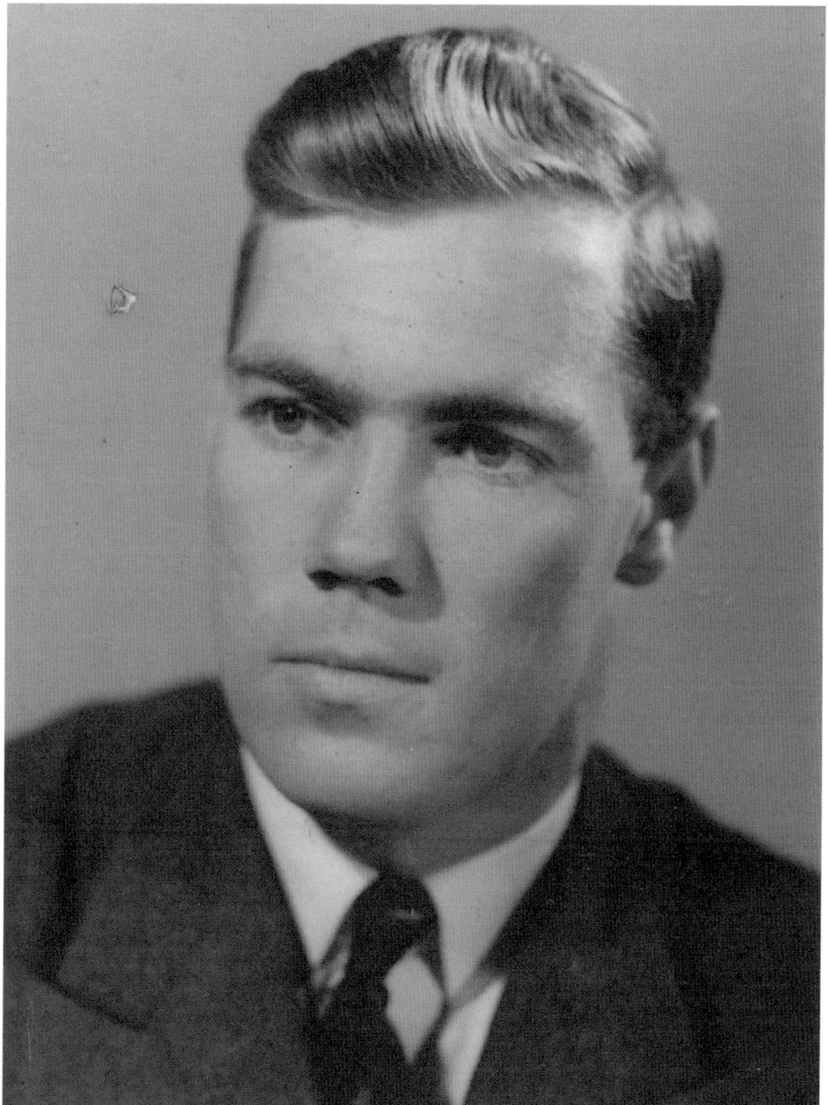

At Oxford, 1952

4 ADVENTURES IN KENYA

At first, I was posted to an administrative role in a comparatively peaceful area of central Kenya.

Administrators were often referred to as 'Jacks of all trades and masters of none'. As I settled in, I realised that comment had a certain ring of truth. The role encompassed a huge range of responsibilities and required a number of skills. In a way, you couldn't really prepare for it. You simply had to train 'on the job'.

The area was inhabited by the Maasai people. I spent much of my time attempting to mobilise almost-naked warriors to hunt down Mau Mau gangs in the area. Unfortunately, they seemed far more interested in eating meat, looking for honey and sleeping with the girls. After one abortive hunt for the Mau Mau, we arrived at a Maasai village and all the girls came out. As a great honour, I was offered one strapping lass who was covered in red ochre and sheep fat. I declined, not least because her husband was the butcher who supplied my meat.

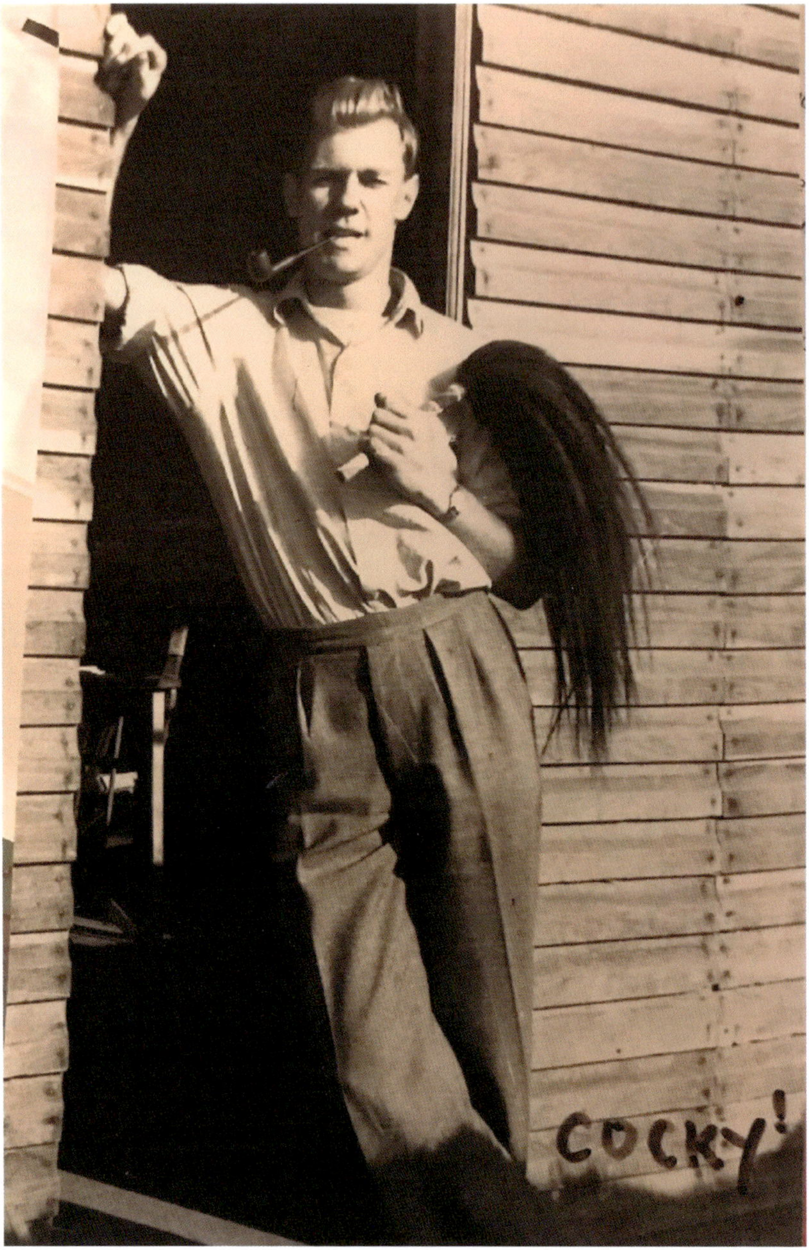
COCKY!

In Kenya

Narok District Maasailand, Kenya

With the Maasai in the Narok district

The Maasai took my breath away. Like so many, I succumbed completely to Maasai-itis, a kind of rock-solid conviction that their way of life was almost perfect and should not be interfered with.

I took hundreds of photographs of the people and their rituals. Their ancient and unique culture completely got under my skin, so much so that I became the only administrative officer to get a distinction in the Maasai language.

Thereby hangs a tale. The night before the exam, I got drunk at a local bar called Hoppy's Inn. On the way home, I overturned my government-issue Land Rover and wrote it off! Amazingly, I was unhurt. Next morning, nursing a hangover, I went into a room with the American missionary who was conducting the exam and after a while, I saw through the window the mangled remains of my Land Rover being taken away. I pointed at the wreck and said in my most unctuous Maasai, "Oh look. Thanks be to God I'm still here!" The missionary was so impressed with my fluency; she gave me a distinction. A case of snatching triumph from the jaws of disaster, if ever there was one.

In 1955, after just two years, I was posted away to Kikuyuland where the Mau Mau conflict was still in progress. I was to take over Kandara division in the Central Province, a far more senior post than I could have expected. The previous incumbent had been killed in a car crash with his wife, a tragedy quite unconnected to the Mau Mau conflict.

Amongst other duties, I was frequently sent into the forest with a police patrol to try to flush out the Mau Mau rebels and engage them in battle. We seldom made contact. The rebels would hear our car engines or the elephantine tramp of the Kenyan police from miles away, and duly scatter.

In recent years I have read allegations of torture and cruelty towards Mau Mau prisoners in that era. I can honestly say I never saw anything of the kind, as I had no responsibility for the detention camps in my divisions. They came under another department altogether.

A year later, I was posted to another division – Kigumo. While I was there, I took the decision to adopt a Kikuyu child called Mary. I had no relatives of my own, and felt I needed at least one, so I paid Mary's mother to look after her and provided for her education. She was bright and did well.

Eventually, I sent her on a secretarial course in London for two years after which she got a good job as secretary to a managing director in Nairobi. In due course she had two daughters of her own, and visited me in my later years in Dorset.

While I was serving in another area called Limuru, Aunt Vi died. On hearing the news in my office, I leapt to my feet and shouted, "I'm free, I'm free!". I feel a little ashamed to admit it now. After all, Vi had done so much for me. But my upbringing had not been straightforward and, as per Vi's wishes, I had been compelled to spend all my leave driving her around in a little car she bought for the purpose, so I certainly had mixed feelings. As it turned out, I was unable to go back to England for her funeral, so I never got the chance to say goodbye.

Mary, my adopted Kenyan daughter

Life went on. The work in Limuru entailed travelling around the divisions keeping in touch with local chiefs and acting as a third-class magistrate dealing with minor cases. Whilst there, I did something that no other district officer had ever had to do. There was a strike at the local Bata shoe factory. I went in the back of a police Land Rover right into the middle of a protest that was beginning to spiral out of control. As a magistrate I read the Riot Act aloud in Swahili. Only then were the police empowered to take action against the rioters. I was genuinely scared, but that act had the desired effect and, thankfully, the crowd began to disperse.

At Fort Hall Kenya, Klambu district, with Senior Chief N'jiiri

Map of Mandera

My next posting was district commissioner in Mandera, a region in the remote north-east of Kenya, 600 miles from Nairobi. The nearest doctor was 250 miles away, so we made do with a dispensary and an African dresser, who performed marvels with the few drugs he had at his disposal. As time went on, I learned that the most common ailments he treated were crocodile bites and the clap.

Mandera district bordered on two international frontiers, Somalia and Ethiopia. It was relatively peaceful but because of its size, 15,000 square miles, the job meant going out on safari a great deal. Indeed, you were required to be out of the district HQ for a minimum of ten days a month and were also supposed to complete 100 miles each month on foot or camel.

There was a grazing boundary in Mandera called the Somali Line, which had been imposed by the British to deter Somali tribes from crossing into other parts of Kenya. We had to set up armed patrols to enforce the line. This was meant to prevent encroachment by stock into non-Somali tribal grazing areas, a problem which had the potential to trigger inter-tribal clashes.

Travel was mainly in Land Rovers but occasionally we went on camel to more remote areas to engage with the locals and 'show the flag'. Our animals were equipped with wooden saddles topped with cushions. Sitting atop a camel meant your thighs were parallel with the ground so you couldn't grip with your knees, as you would on a horse. A camel walks at around two to three miles an hour, which is quite relaxing, until they decide to trot, at which point you bounce painfully. After riding a camel for 100 miles, I developed a large boil on my rump and was forced to walk the return journey – much to the amusement of my Somali tribal police escort. The Somalis like to say, 'First God made the land; next he made the Somali; and after that, the camel – and then he laughed'.

Despite the discomfort of such journeys, there were many benefits to safari, not least the opportunity to sleep the night under the stars. I remember seeing Sputnik orbiting over our campsite one night, as well as a number of passenger planes – the onboard cocktails and stewardesses way beyond our reach.

My least favourite mode of transport, Mandera

Whilst I was in Mandera, a herdsman brought in three lion cubs. His fellow herdsmen had been forced to kill the mother because she had been eating their cattle, no doubt to feed her cubs. The question was, what did we do with them? I contacted George and Joy Adamson, who lived in Kenya and had been immortalised by the book and film, *Born Free*, for advice. The upshot was that I kept the most adorable cub and asked the Kenya police to shoot the other two. It may seem unduly harsh but we were in the bush, 600 miles from Nairobi, and I could not possibly cope with all three.

I called my cub Sheba. We became the best of friends. I often played with her, getting down on the floor and romping around as you would with any friendly cat.

Sheba, the lioness cub

As you can imagine, there comes a point when the owner of a lioness cub begins to question their choice of pet – and their future! Sheba was well fed and grew rapidly. I could not take her on my safaris and often had to leave her with my bearer or cook. After a few months she grew larger. One day she knocked me over while we were playing. I can picture the moment clearly. She stood over me but didn't know what to do next. Luckily her mother had not had time to tell her! I managed to push her off me and get up before she figured it out.

I loved Sheba but mutual trust had now been broken. So, we built a large cage for her outside so she wasn't tempted to eat her owner whilst roaming the house. I offered her to Sir Hugh Garrard Tyrwhitt-Drake, the owner of Whipsnade Zoo and he agreed to take her. But he wanted me to arrange for her air freight to England, which was going to cost me £80. This was roughly equivalent to two months' salary. As she was growing fast, and the locals were afraid she might escape, I hardened my heart and asked the police chief to shoot her while I went off on safari. It was a very sad moment for me, even more so for my cook with whom she had formed a special bond.

As a district commissioner, I was also a first-class magistrate. The extra powers that went with this role were needed if it was necessary to hear preliminary enquiries into serious matters like murder, or when it was necessary to impose heavy fines. One day the senior Kenya police officer in the district brought in a very beautiful young teenage Somali prostitute who had been charged with aggravated trespass. He said she kept coming across the international Kenya/Somalia frontier half a mile away to ply her trade on the police lines. Unfortunately, this caused friction between members of the police Askaris, who all fought for her favours. The police officer claimed that however many times she was sent back over the border, she always returned. He made a request – that, if I found her guilty, I would send her away to serve her sentence at the women's prison in Nairobi, some 600 miles away. The prison was home to many prostitutes. It was a slightly tricky issue as the girl was not a Kenyan citizen, but it was clear her repeated crime was causing a serious problem. So, I ignored the issue of her nationality and sentenced her to three months in prison in Nairobi.

On hearing this, she burst into tears. "Oh, sir," she pleaded. "Please don't send me to Nairobi as the people there are Kufaar (non Muslim) and cannibals. You are sentencing me to death."

I tried to reassure the girl that she would be completely safe, but she would not be comforted. She was taken away sobbing and put on the next transport to Nairobi, a journey of two days.

About 11 weeks later I received an order from the Supreme Court that quashed my sentence. I was ordered to have the girl returned to Mandera and deported over the frontier with a clean record! On arrival, she was brought before me to be told of her acquittal. "Oh, sir," she said, in a much brighter mood than when I'd last seen her, "I want to thank you for sending me down to Nairobi. I learnt so many new things from the women in prison there which will be so useful to me now I am home." It turned out that, in her case, prison had been an education!

While I was serving as a district commissioner in the Northern Province, I had to conduct a referendum of all the Somalis (around 200,000) in my district. The British had promised to give them a choice over whether they wanted to join Somalia after independence or stay in Kenya. As one of the six district commissioners in the Northern Frontier, I was told to encourage the people to vote exactly as they pleased without fear of any consequences – even if they wanted secession from Kenya. Above all, the people were assured that their wishes would be respected and that a decision would be given before the granting of internal self- government to Kenya's African majority.

Independence for Kenya was a matter of time and the Somalis understandably wanted no part of it. They all voted to join Somalia. As it turned out later, the newly independent Kenyan government refused to enact the promise given by the British, fearing the country's borders would be compromised – as indeed they would have been.

In my opinion, the referendum had been a delaying tactic by the British to keep the Somalis quiet until they could hand over to the independent Kenyan government, knowing full well it would never allow the Somalis to secede! I had believed, perhaps naively, the Kenyan government would honour its pledge, although in hindsight, I can see that a new country would hardly agree to give away a large part of its territory. But to Somalia – and Somalis – this felt like double-dealing.

In 1963, I went back to the UK on leave. Many district commissioners were by now pretty disillusioned by the breaking of assurances made to the Somalis and had decided they did not want to serve under an independent Kenyan government. I wasn't averse to staying on, so I hadn't yet handed in my notice. But after just three months of the six I'd been hoping to enjoy, I was recalled 'in the national interest'.

My orders were very clear. I was to return to Mandera and convince the Somalis that they could not secede. Utterly ashamed of the way this had been handled, I flatly refused to go back to Mandera. I had three meetings with the permanent secretary to the governor's office in Nairobi. At first, he flattered me. I spoke Somali, knew Mandera, and was trusted by the Somalis. When that failed, he appealed to my reason. Had I really thought that Kenyan Somalis would be allowed to secede? Wouldn't the map of Kenya look rather strange if they did? When that didn't work, he started to threaten me with dismissal without a pension. Was it worth forfeiting that for Somalis, they asked – such a costly gesture, which would achieve nothing?

Looking back, I must admit that there was an element of self-preservation in my refusal to go. It was my skin at risk, not theirs.

Eventually, after appeals to my loyalty and further pressure, I finally relented and returned to Mandera, but only after giving six months' notice.

Grim news greeted me in Mandera. One of the first African district commissioners, a chief who had been in charge of Isiolo, had been killed. I was told by Special Branch that the man's killers had been dispatched from Mogadishu with instructions to eliminate me too. In fact, they were now in a village just across the Somali border, about 1,000 yards from my house. The border was merely another overgrown line cut through the bush. I felt very vulnerable. I had a pistol, but that would not have been much use against a Sten gun. My armed police escort gave me some comfort. Somalis may be individualistic and fiercely loyal to their clan, but they also have a great sense of personal loyalty and I knew he would have defended me with his life.

As it turned out, another escort had lost his life defending a fellow district commissioner, Ken Arnold, when he was killed (and emasculated) a few months later by Somali freedom fighters, known as Shifta rebels.

My first step was to order a batch of leaflets from Nairobi to distribute locally, offering a £2,000 reward for the capture of the two killers – dead or alive. But in the meantime, I was becoming very edgy. There was little stopping the two men crossing the border and shooting me dead.

At last the leaflets arrived. I sent men across the border to scatter them. It worked like a charm. To a poor nomad, £2,000 was a small fortune – enough to buy a herd of camels. All they had to do was knock the assassins on the head and drag their bodies over the border. In the end, the killers fled back to Mogadishu.

That was one problem out the way. Others remained. The whole district was still seething about the way it had been treated. It fell to me to convince the locals that they couldn't secede and that they had to remain in Kenya. I also needed to persuade them that it would be in their best interests to take part in elections for a regional assembly before independence. If they chose not to vote, they'd have no voice afterwards.

Feelings ran so high at 'barazas' (public meetings that were mostly held in the bush), my tribal police escort had to form a ring around me with rifles cocked. On one occasion, they were forced to fire into the air to discourage enraged clansmen from attacking us. Had we not made them deposit their spears before the meeting, I'm confident we would have been skewered. I later heard that Radio Mogadishu had attacked me by name on the air, just before the meeting, urging people to rise up against the Europeans.

Mines were laid on roads in an attempt to kill us. We took to travelling in a Twin Pioneer aircraft or an Alouette helicopter. On the night of Kenya's independence, 12th December 1963, a rumour spread that Somalia was going to attack Mandera from across the border. We took this with a pinch of salt as, in my experience, Somalis were great rumour-mongers. Nonetheless, both the Kenya Rifles and Kenya police stood by.

Nothing happened. We all had a drink and then lowered the Union Jack, which we signed.

Four weeks later, the European district commissioner in the neighbouring district of Wajir was shot dead. He was only a temporary relief for the substantive DC who was on leave. Unaware of the risks, he had stood in front of his tent, silhouetted by the light of a pressure lamp – presenting a clear target for a sniper in the dark.

We criticised the Kenya Rifles for failing to catch the Shifta, or being scared of them. In fact, some of the soldiers sympathised with them. The only Somali they shot was a nine-year-old cattle herder, whom they claimed was a Shifta. The authorities in Kenya ordered me to hold an inquest into the boy's death. This was just a couple of months before my leaving date and it gave me pause for thought. An inquest that implicated the Kenyan troops in the murder of an innocent child was not going to go down well and would be lengthy.

Sure enough, the Kenyan soldiers were furious at this possibility. One of the non-Somali members of the platoon sent a message to warn me not to walk to my office in future as if I did, I would get shot by a Kenyan Somali soldier. I could already imagine the kind of excuse that would have been offered in that instance – how a soldier had been cleaning his rifle and accidentally pulled the trigger. It was bad enough being targeted by assassins and the Shifta. To be targeted by my own troops was the final indignity.

I heeded the warning and, from then on, drove to the office in the Land Rover every day. It was a tense time. And, after handing over to my successor four months after independence, I heard that the matter of the nine-year-old boy was quietly dropped. A tragedy for his family.

As soon as my six months' notice period was up, I knew it was time to go. For the next three years, the Somalis in the region conducted a bitter guerrilla campaign to try and secure independence from Kenya. They failed. The Kenyan army was far more ruthless than anyone had anticipated. Unable to catch the guerrillas, they opted instead to shoot civilians by the hundreds, as well as decimate stock.

Considering this sad period in British history, it is easy to conclude that colonialism was a huge disaster. Not so, in my opinion. In under a century, we had brought peace and with it, development, education and improved healthcare. It's possibly true to say that the Westminster model of democracy might not have been suitable for some of the tribal societies we colonised, but perhaps we did not give that experiment long enough to develop. However, I sincerely believe we gave many countries a structure and stability from which they benefited then and, to an extent, even today.

5 HEAT, DUST AND CHAOS IN ADEN

I was keen not to return to the UK without a job. As it turned out, I needn't have worried. I was soon heading straight to my next adventure – as a political officer in Aden.

Aden was in a state of chaos. An armed insurgency, known as the Aden Emergency, had begun a year earlier against British forces stationed in South Arabia. It was a sensitive time.

The posting was tough in other respects. The landscape was harsh, barren and uninspiring, and the climate unforgiving. There was barely any shade anywhere, no parks or greenery to soak up the heat. Hideous sandstorms frequently battered the country, leaving grit in every corner of the house.

Seeking recreation in such an environment wasn't easy. But it was in Aden that I first met Anne Doe, a young woman who had grown up in Kenya. She was a formidable tennis and squash player – so good, in fact, that she played for the Aden Men's Squash Team. Indeed, she beat me at squash that first time we met, quite a tough defeat to swallow as I'd always thought I was rather good at it.

I found her very attractive and we soon became friends, although at the time she was married with two young children, Charles and Rowena.

Initially, I had wanted to go to the Eastern Aden Protectorate, because of its reputation as 'a wild and woolly' place of nomadic herders, camels, mountains and wadis. But instead I was sent to Dhala, in the Western Aden Protectorate, while the incumbent political officer, James Nash (an embryonic 'Lawrence of Arabia' type) took some leave. Like every political officer who served in Dhala, his residence, a white-washed fort, was regularly shot up by dissidents. The night I arrived to take up residence, the same thing happened to me. I remember receiving what was intended as a consoling piece of advice. "Sahib," one staff member said. "Don't worry. They'll never hit you unless you stand up in plain sight."

My nerves were soon calmed. It transpired that every new arrival got this hostile reception, a reminder to the British that dissidents were also in residence and we would never be completely in charge.

Dhala covered an area close to the border with Yemen, where there was civil war. One of the jobs I inherited from James was to hand out rifles and ammunition to one side of the conflict, the Yemeni Royalists, so they could 'shoot up' the opposing Egyptian backed faction. As it turned out, although they claimed to have engaged with the Egyptian army, they more often than not simply shot bullets into a hillside. Needless to say, they always came back for more supplies.

Another of my tasks was to give financial support to chosen Yemeni tribes. I did this by making hand-outs of Maria Teresa thalers (silver bullion coins which were first minted in Austria in 1741 and, by this stage, were used as trade currency across the Arab world). The coins I used were minted in Birmingham and, despite being the real deal, were always initially viewed with suspicion by the Yemenis. However, once they had bitten the coin and were satisfied it was made of silver, they were happy enough.

When James returned from leave, I went back to Aden and was then transferred to be assistant advisor to the local Sultan in a rural state called Wahidi, to the north east of Aden.

The Sultan was a nasty bandy-legged little man whose despot of a state secretary, Mohamed Bin Said, effectively ran the state for him. There was no love lost between them. Bin Said would often call the Sultan a dog, but just out of earshot.

In addition to her prowess on the squash court, Anne Doe had a great talent as a watercolourist. Seeking inspiration outside Aden she came up to Wahidi with another artist friend to stay in the agricultural officer's empty house in Maifa'a, Wahidi's state capital.

No-one had told me she was coming, and I was very cross when I found her walking in the souk without an escort. I asked her what she was doing there without any protection. Anne contended that she spoke Arabic, had been around a lot longer than I had and women were not at risk like I was. I realised that she was more than able to take care of herself. It was a pleasure to have her around and her visit was all too short.

Mohamed Bin Said, State Secretary, Wahidi

One day in 1965 I received a terse message from the Assistant High Commissioner: 'The Deiyyin and the Mashajera are at it again. Visit Yeb'eth and investigate.'

The Deiyyin and the Mashajera were two tribes living on either side of what was then the border between the Eastern Aden Protectorate and the former Western Aden Protectorate, now the Federation of South Arabia, of which Wahidi State was a new member.

That the two tribes were shooting at each other once again was nothing new. They were always doing it, and now and again somebody actually got killed. It was their form of recreation. Small wonder they built their houses with bullet- proof, thick walls and slit windows.

Maifa'a, the capital of Wahidi State where I was stationed, was only 50 miles from Yeb'eth. But with no connecting roads, the journey was far from straightforward – only for the truly curious and determined.

Freya Stark was one of a handful of Europeans who had visited. She had written a memorable account of the experience in her book, *A Winter in Arabia*. This made it all the more tantalising.

I arranged for baggage camels to be hired from some nearby tribesmen to meet us at a well-known as Bir al Masaijit. My Arab assistant adviser Abdulqadir, my Somali cook Yusuf, and an escort of some 15 federal guardsmen collected the necessary food and equipment for a two-week trip. We then set off up the wadi, or dry riverbed, in two Land Rovers to meet the camels.

One of the subsidiary aims of my visit to Yeb'eth was to reconnoitre a possible route for a road. I only told a few of our party. Had the owners of the baggage camels known, they might not have been willing to hire them out, as their livelihood depended on there being no road.

As we were late in arriving, we found that the herdsmen had taken most of the camels off to graze. The trek had to be made at night to avoid the intense heat.

As it was only afternoon we camped at the well and I and three young federal guardsmen raced to the top of a nearby hill for exercise and to see the view. When I told them where we were going they all offered to fight the Deiyyin, a generous offer I had to decline, albeit with thanks. All of them came from tribes in the Western Aden Protectorate, which made them marginally more sympathetic to the Mashajera side of the conflict.

Back in camp we supped and prepared the loads for the baggage camels before settling down for an early sleep ready to strike camp at two in the morning. During the night a heavy dew fell. When we woke, everything was wet. After loading the protesting camels, we set off up the rocky wadi illuminated only by moonlight.

The Sultan of Wahidi State had sent along his representative for the forthcoming negotiations. He was a wily old fox who was always making facetious jokes. He was also extremely lazy.

Prior to starting out, a roll was called. He was the only absentee. We thought that maybe he was still asleep but after poking around the rocks, we heard a chuckling voice from high up asked what we were looking for. And there he was, perched on the only riding camel in the whole bunch.

Our first stop was to be at Dhirra an Naws (the Rock of the Fruitless Date Palm) some five hours away. We were now travelling through an extremely inhospitable landscape. There is no water in the region, except during the very short rainy period in October – then a month away. From Dhirra, our route lay to Saiq (seven hours), Kalab (six hours) and finally Yeb'eth (three hours). Laden-baggage camels can generally walk up to two-and-a-half miles an hour but some of the going was uphill in the dark and some downhill, which was even slower, so it was impossible to accurately gauge how quickly we would cover the ground.

Bored by their slow pace we edged past the camels in the dark and struck out ahead, the black cliffs of the wadi towering above us in the moonlight. By six o'clock, dawn was near and we climbed out of the wadi and reached the pass known as Aqabat Aabit Nahadha. The sun began to rise and soon burst over the crest to our right throwing our giant shadows across the hillside. We left a walkie-talkie set with the camel escort and pressed on to Dhirra an Naws. Our food was with the camels so we had to wait until they arrived before we could have breakfast.

We reached Yeb'eth two days later where we were met by Mashajera tribesmen firing a zaamil – a welcoming fusillade of shots – over our heads.

That journey was far more memorable than the actual mission. The visit was a success in a way – the fighting stopped, if only temporarily, as we pulled the two tribes together and got them to talk. But it was the experience of being in that extraordinary landscape that has stayed with me.

When my posting in Wahidi ended, I handed over to a British army major and flew back to Aden. It was to prove a narrow escape. A week later, my successor was on another flight to Aden. This time, the Sultan had given his own orderly a briefcase containing a bomb. It was intended to kill his hated State Secretary. The plan was that the plane would blow up over the sea, no bodies would be recovered, and no one would know there had ever been a bomb on board. As it turned out, the bomb exploded over land, and the plot was exposed. Everyone on board died, including my successor.

It was a deeply shocking event. And I couldn't help thinking, *there but for the grace of God went I.*

When my contract ended, I decided to return to the UK. In my period in Aden, I had served as a political officer in the Western and Eastern Aden Protectorates. For a short time, I also acted as private secretary to Sir Richard Turnbull, the governor of Aden, in Government House. I was sad to leave.

Looking back, I regretted leaving the colonial service because it had been deeply satisfying. I enjoyed the open-air life in wild, untamed landscapes like Kenya and Aden. Being a district officer, getting to know the locals and attempting to help them find way to resolve problems was the best job I've had in my life.

In full colonial service rig

6 WORKING FOR AUNTIE

In 1967, I arrived back in the UK with no real idea about what I should do next. As luck would have it, I heard about a vacancy in the Somali Service at BBC Bush House. Given my grasp of the language, I thought I was in with a chance, and applied. To my delight, I got the job.

With the BBC Somali Service

It was a very good move on my part. Over the years, I progressed from language supervisor and producer, to programme organiser. But beyond career progression, my time at the BBC was rich in so many other ways.

It was our job at the Somali Service to follow every event in Somalia. This was rarely straightforward. Carved up by clans, the country had spawned no less than 63 political parties. In 1969, elections and indeed democracy went out of the window with the military coup spearheaded by General Mohamed Siad Barre, who later invited the Russians in to bolster his position. In the short term, his decision seemed the right one, as the Russians helped to arm him. But then in 1977, when the General declared war on Ethiopia in an attempt to capture the Ogaden region, his Russian allies swapped sides and gained the foothold in Ethiopia they had craved in the last century. Not only was Somalia defeated, it was destabilised. It was never reunited again.

Despite these sad developments, my job was deeply satisfying. I loved Bush House in the Strand, which was such a warm and friendly place, with a wonderful multiracial atmosphere. The corporation arranged for me to attend the School of Oriental and African Studies to study advanced Somali, so I was able to fine tune my skills. And in 1971, I was sent to attend an amazing seminar held in Salzburg, on 'The US, Europe and the Developing World.' Later on, I was despatched to Mogadishu where I met the notorious Siad Barre. He was very friendly towards me, no doubt because of the power and influence of the BBC World Service, but we all knew he was a dictator. Quite how much of a dictator only emerged later, when it became clear his 21-year rule had been characterised by the widespread persecution, jailing and torture of political opponents and dissidents, and thousands of deaths.

Aunt Vi was by now long gone so I was free to live my life. I bought a flat in Baron's Court in West London and had a great time going to plays, concerts, opera and ballet – cultural experiences I had been starved of in my 14 years in Somaliland, Kenya and Aden. I bought a souped-up Mini Cooper Special and drove it around Britain, getting to know the country I had missed.

In 1967, my friend Anne Doe returned to England to set up home in Dorset. Her husband, Brian, remained in Aden. I knew that their marriage was pretty rocky, but I later learned from friends in Aden that 'another woman' had joined Brian out there.

I felt it was my duty(!) to inform Anne about this extra woman. So, I drove to Dorset to deliver the news. What I told her 'cast the die'. She decided to start divorce proceedings against Brian and bought a small cottage at 103 Newland, in Sherborne.

We did not see much of each other after that. I was occupied in London with my job at the BBC. Anne went on to marry again, and for the time being, we kept in touch only through Christmas cards.

After seven years working at the BBC, I felt it was time to move on and looked around for another challenge. Given my love of far-flung, exotic destinations, it was little surprise that I was soon heading abroad again.

7 A LAST ADVENTURE IN HONG KONG

In 1974, I was offered a post in Hong Kong as a district officer. I arrived to find that all business was conducted in Cantonese, which made it almost impossible for me to understand what was going on. I protested that the job needed a Cantonese-speaking officer and, while they found me another role, it did not seem like a promising start.

I went on to work in several government secretariat jobs, including the Department of Trade Industry and Customs, and acted as clerk to the Hong Kong Executive Council, which was chaired by the Governor. I ended up as civil secretary for the fire services department. While some of the work was quite dull, Hong Kong as a place was always exciting – a colony full of energy and frisson.

Despite the fact I was a single man, I was allocated large married quarters on the Peak of Hong Kong Island, where I lived with my cats, Bonny and Nikko, and my devoted Filipina amah (or housekeeper) Gloria Valenzuela, with whom I am still in touch. The flat had unrivalled views across to Kowloon. Morning and evening, I commuted on the antiquated Peak Tram. I became a member of the Ladies' Recreation Club (where, rather confusingly, male members were also allowed to join), a comfortable colonial- era club where men and women enjoyed sports facilities and a swimming pool. Best of all, I joined a multi-racial rambling group which went on long walks around Hong Kong, Kowloon, the New Territories and nearby islands – nearly every weekend - until I retired.

With Gloria and the cats in the flat

Hiking in the Hong Kong hills

I heard from Anne again. By now, her second husband Malcolm Moorse had died. I invited her to come and stay with me. She stayed for a fortnight, joining me on my rambles or painting the old, teeming back streets of the colony, capturing their chaos and vitality wonderfully.

Shortly afterwards, my personal life took another surprising turn.

Despite several attempts at tracing my birth mother, I had had no success. But then, in February 1982, when I was 51 years old, I received a long airmail letter from a woman called Deirdre Curwen, who lived in Lancashire. She said she was my sister and told me that I had seven other living relatives – my mother Muriel, a second sister Audrey Steer, a niece Lesley Curwen, three nephews, David, Andrew and Keith Steer, and a brother-in-law Tony Steer.

As you can imagine, it was quite a shock. Until that day, I wasn't sure my birth mother was even alive. It had never occurred to me that I had siblings, let alone an extended family.

Once I'd made contact, Audrey then sent a 54-page letter, describing her own adoption and traumatic childhood.

It emerged that my sister, Deirdre, had been placed with elderly adoptive parents at just 10 days old. Audrey, the youngest, had been fostered several times and was finally adopted at the age of four. After the birth of Audrey, it seems our mother, Muriel, had a nervous breakdown. She finished her affair with Hubert Archibald King, tore up his letters and photos, and never saw him again.

After receiving these momentous (and enormous) missives, I flew back to the UK to meet my new family. My sisters and their children welcomed me warmly, the first blood relatives I had ever met, apart from those earliest memories of my birth mother. I was introduced, almost at a stroke, to eight people who were kin. It's one thing being told you have all these relatives. It's quite another meeting them. I met Lesley first, at Richmond Tube Station. I didn't know what she looked like, nor she me. I seem to remember her approaching me and asking if I was Mr Walker. At first there were nerves, and a little distance. It was a scary experience for us both. But we went for a long walk in the park and by the end of the day, the ice had been broken.

I finally met Muriel Rogers in 1983, at her cottage in Hook, Hampshire. I was 52. It was not a warm occasion. I felt no closeness to her at all. I don't think I remembered her as the woman who'd delivered me to the spinsters. It was like a piece of fiction, as if I were an actor in a play, rather than an active participant.

Muriel confessed that she wanted to borrow £5,000 from me to pay off a mortgage on her cottage. I lent her the money but didn't expect her to pay it back. It's fair to say I didn't trust her. Fifty years had elapsed and at no point had she thought to let me know I had siblings. In the end, she did pay me back. She died two years later, and I was not able to attend her funeral.

None of my family had ever made contact with Hubert Archibald King or his children, even though some of those descendants have been identified through genealogy searches. One of Muriel's few surviving black and white photos is said to be of Hubert, though his face is in deep shadow.

My mother, Muriel, 1983

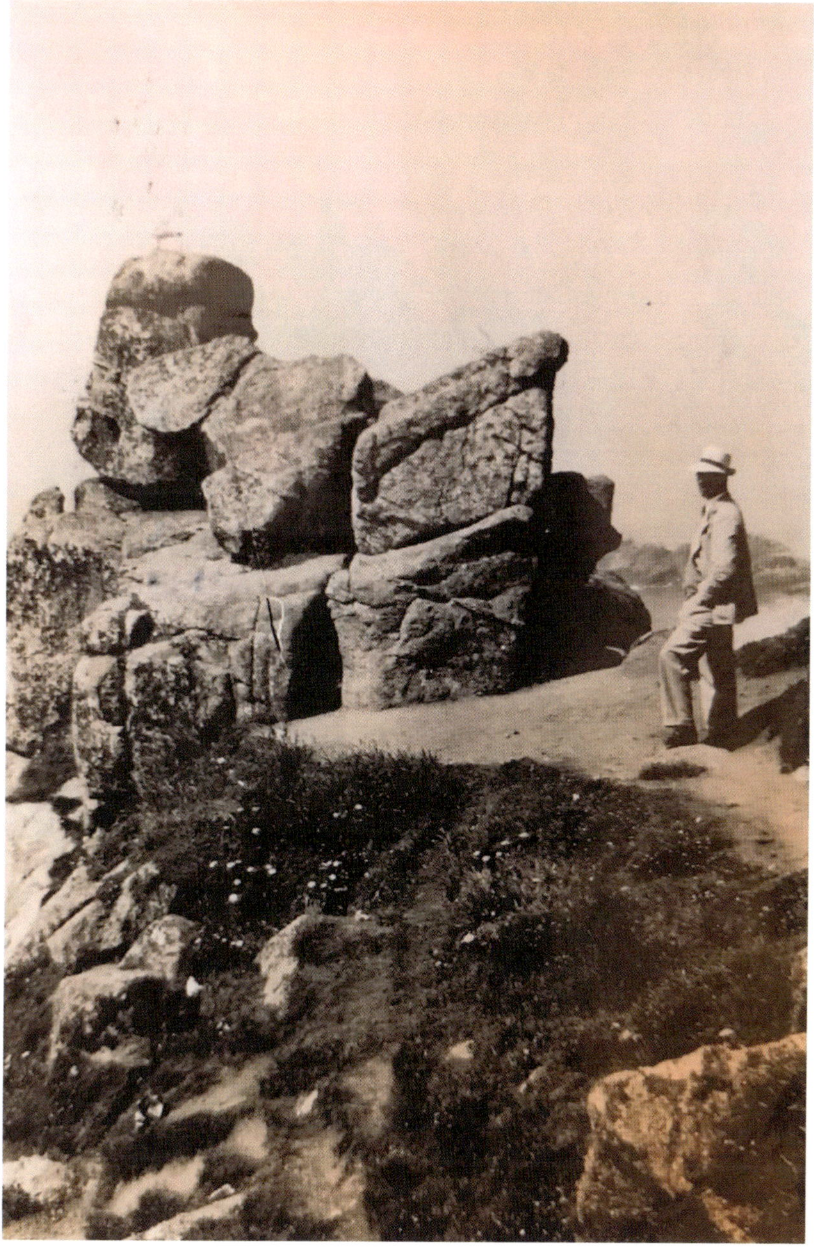

The faceless father

A new era began where I spent much of my leave from Hong Kong visiting my long-lost family at their homes in Preston, London and Market Bosworth. The family also travelled en masse to see my old friends, Josefina and Delmar, Banner in the Lakes. Josefina was delighted and thought it was 'the happiest story ever' that the siblings had found each other. Gradually, Audrey, Deirdre and I got to know each other better. We were all prolific writers and many airmail letters flew between the UK and Hong Kong. I was able to play host to family members at my flat on the Peak. Lesley, who had joined BBC News, visited while on assignment as a reporter.

With my sisters and Josefina

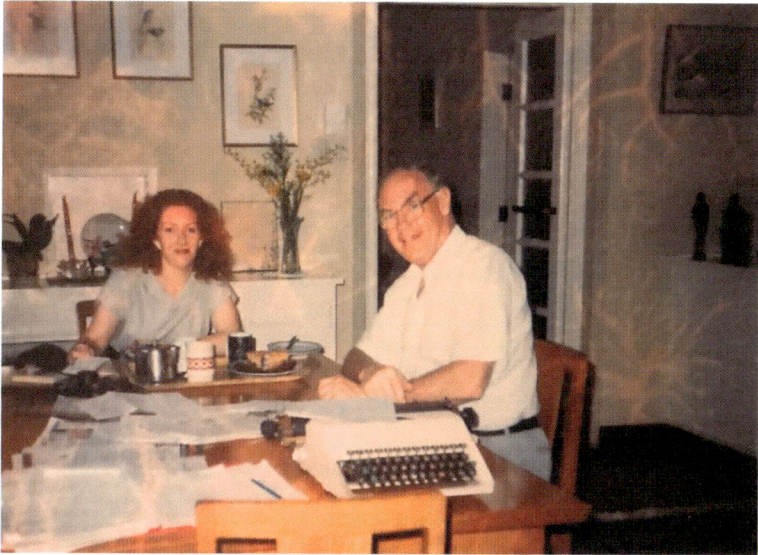

Lesley at the Peak apartment, 1986

My sisters leaving Hong Kong for home, October 1987

Receiving my MBE, flanked by my sisters

In 1987, I received an MBE from the Queen for my 28 years of work in the colonial service. I invited both my sisters to be guests at the ceremony in Buckingham Palace. It was a wonderful moment.

The photo shows Deirdre and Audrey glowing with pride, next to me, dressed in the usual top hat and tails. I was overheard to jest that MBE stood for 'My Bloody Efforts', while OBE stands for 'Other Buggers' Efforts'.

A year later, in May 1988, my employment contract was not renewed, and I had to retire from my civil service job in Hong Kong at the age of 57.

Having left Hong Kong, it was time to find another job. This time I compiled a proper C.V., with the expert help of my sister,

Deirdre, who typed it up. The C.V. records that my languages now included fluent Swahili, some Somali, elementary Arabic and colloquial Cantonese. It turns out that, despite my problems at school, I was quite the linguist! The C.V. was sent to various advertising agencies, but in the end, I opted for another short-term contract in Hong Kong. This role involved hearing the appeals of Vietnamese boat people who had entered Hong Kong illegally and left me with the heavy burden of deciding whether individuals were genuine refugees or economic migrants.

I rented an apartment in the heart of Wan Chai in the mid-levels of Hong Kong Island. It was a modest space with just enough room for visitors. Lesley came out on another work trip, which was wonderful. My old friend Anne also paid a visit. To my delight, she stayed for three months. She painted prolifically, her watercolours capturing all the vibrancy and colour of the colony's back streets and markets. Towards the end of her time in Hong Kong, Anne exhibited her work. It was received with great enthusiasm and she sold every single painting.

Dealing with the cases of Vietnamese boat people was incredibly stressful. Looking back, I can say with certainty that this was the most intense job I had ever done. I heard so many sad stories and felt in an impossible position. My Chinese colleagues were adamant that most if not all of them were illegal, and that none deserved to stay. But I just couldn't take that attitude. I would dearly have liked to allow their appeals but more often than not, there were no grounds for me to do so.

In the end I found the pressure of work too much and, in 1992, I decided to return home to the UK for good.

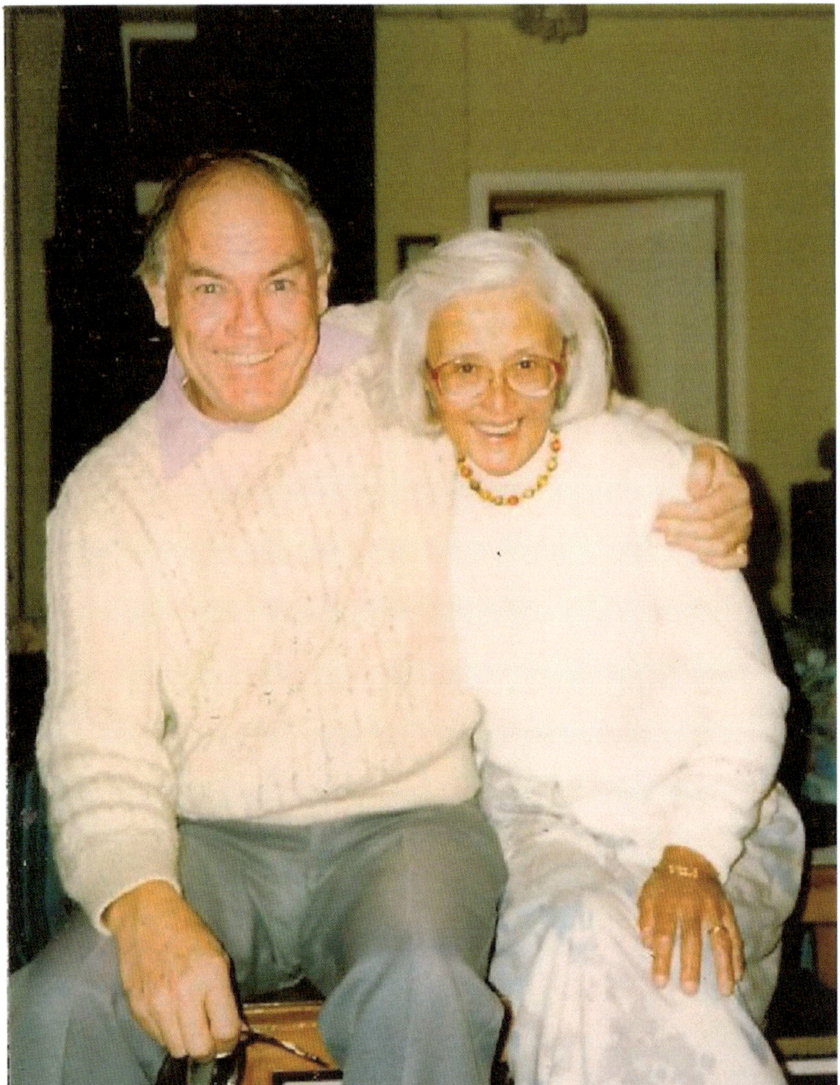

With Anne in Hong Kong

8 SETTLING IN SHERBORNE

After years of living as a colonial ex-patriate, I was finally home. Anne kindly invited me to stay with her in her house in Sherborne in Dorset, so I let my London flat and moved to the West Country. It's been my home ever since.

We lived together for four years. Then one day we were driving through a village called Long Burton. I stopped the car outside a church, turned to Anne and asked if she would like to marry me. I was overjoyed when she said 'yes'. That place has remained very precious to us. Whenever we pass, we remember that happy day.

On 5th September 1997, aged 66, I married Anne. At a stroke, I became a member of another loving and close family. I have been stepfather to Anne's children, Rowena and Charles, and step-grandfather to Hamish, Cameron and Catriona, and the twins, Genevieve and Archie.

It might surprise you to hear that I settled into life in Sherborne. You might assume that a man who'd had so many adventures would crave more. I think the opposite was true. I welcomed stability. I was well into my sixties, but in reality, Anne's house was the first settled home I'd ever known. I'd been on the move for decades. It was time to stay still.

On our wedding day, with Charles, Catriona and Hamish

David, Rowena, Catriona, Hamish and Cameron

With Charles, Gail, Anne, Archie and Genevieve

Sherborne is a wonderful place to do just that, with a wealth of opportunities to get involved in the community. I volunteered with local charities like the British Legion and the Citizens Advice Bureau, although I was hopeless when it came to offering advice on the benefits system, which I found impenetrable. I also became a sidesman in Sherborne Abbey for church services, directing people to their seats.

My wanderlust needed the occasional sating. Anne and I visited Oman and Jordan – an area of the world I loved. Obviously much had changed, not least us. No longer insiders, we were now viewing the region through the slightly sanitised spectacles of a tourist. But the trips were fascinating nonetheless and, once again, Anne painted frenetically.

I also returned to Kenya to see old friends who'd stayed on after independence. It was a rather melancholic experience. It felt like the country had deteriorated a great deal. A once proud and beautiful country appeared to be in a state of decline.

Anne's creativity has been a shared focus for us both. I supported her chairmanship of the Sherborne Art Club for five years and became the club's treasurer for seven years. Her catalogue of work is remarkable. A self-taught watercolourist, she has produced hundreds of works which capture people, the natural world and the bustle of urban life with enormous skill, as well as great wit. I've managed to gather much of it all together for a website showcasing her artistic career, and commissioned the writing and publication of her memoir, which sets out all the experiences that shaped her life as an artist.

Anne's watercolour of Sherborne Abbey

My birth family remains very important to me. My sisters visited me when they could.

In 2010, I was honoured to walk my niece Lesley down the aisle when she married Nic Vine. Having lost my family at an early age only to be reunited so many years later, this was a very special moment for me.

About to walk Lesley down the aisle

Deirdre's 70th birthday, with Audrey, Deirdre
and her two daughters, Lesley and Mary

In 2011, Lesley's mother Deirdre became seriously ill. Audrey and I were able to visit our sister in hospital in London one last time before she died. Having missed out on so much of her life, I was very grateful for the time we had together.

As we've aged, Anne and I have contended with various health challenges. For seven years I cared full-time for her after she was confined to a wheelchair. We may lack the energy we once had but there's plenty around us, with the grandchildren making welcome appearances from time to time.

Looking back on my life, I consider myself to be a very lucky man. Others might think that being put up for adoption isn't an

With Anne

ideal start to life, but from my perspective it provided me with opportunities I would simply not have been afforded otherwise. I was adopted by wealthy spinsters and Aunt Vi ensured I had an excellent education.

I believe the experience of being adopted and then going away to school forged in me a self-reliance. Life with Vi could be a little claustrophobic, but perhaps this persuaded me to take the plunge and accept a role in Somaliland. From then on, I would always seek out fresh adventures and horizons.

Inevitably, after the thrills of Somalia, Kenya, Aden, Hong Kong and other far-flung, exotic places, Sherborne has felt a little quiet. But I have had Anne and her family, as well as the relatives I found later in life, around me. In that respect, I consider myself a lucky man.

AFTERWORD

I have helped my uncle to write this book, along with Story Terrace author, Paddy Magrane, because I really want the story of his life to be told.

Hugh is essentially a modest man, as I realised the first time I met him. I was in my twenties and the first member of our scattered family to meet him face to face. He had just returned on leave from Hong Kong, after receiving a bombshell letter from my mother, which explained that he had two hitherto- unknown sisters, a niece and three nephews.

It was, at first, a rather awkward encounter at Richmond Station. "Are you Mr Walker?" I shyly enquired of the rather stern-looking man in a tweed jacket. But by the end of the afternoon I realised what a perceptive, witty and kind uncle he was. That was almost 40 years ago and since then I have had the joy of getting to know him properly. I still have files full of his neatly hand-written letters, sent to me over the years from Hong Kong and Dorset.

It's only now that I've spent hours talking to him about his extraordinary and hair-raising colonial career, that I understand the great range of heady experiences he tasted. Perhaps that helped to make him the cultured and broad- minded man he is.

Hugh has some qualities in common with his sisters – he is conscientious, energetic and can be quite stubborn. The truth is, he is an unstoppable force, and throughout his eighties, he has been a devoted carer to Anne. He is deeply loved by Anne's family and mine.

From being an unwanted toddler in a children's home, he has become a cherished husband, brother and uncle, stepfather and step-grandfather. That, surely, is the happy ending of his amazing story.

Lesley Curwen, December 2019

Postscript

In September of 2020 Hugh Walker passed away, aged 89. It was cancer that had plagued him for many years, and he had fought it with that spirit and strength that had imbued his whole life.

Just three months later Anne Walker passed away, aged 90. An era seemed to come to a close as their Sherborne cottage, always a place of bustle and noise, fell silent.

Both families hold Hugh and Anne close to their hearts, with loving memories and admiration for all that they achieved in their long lives.

Lesley Curwen & Nic Vine, September 2021

Printed in Great Britain
by Amazon